Dr. Johnson's Apple Orchard

The Story of America's First Pet Cemetery

Dr. Johnson's Apple Orchard

The Story of America's First Pet Cemetery

by Edward C. Martin, Jr.

Dedication

This book is lovingly dedicated to my parents – Edward, who brought me to Hartsdale, a master engraver who spent most of his working life creating magnificent monuments that make the cemetery a showplace of ultimate artistic expression, and Bertha, who for over twenty years received the sorrowful calls of pet-owners and gently explained our procedures with understanding and sensitivity, and whose honest sympathy and respect for their grief I will never forget.

Acknowledgements

This book would not have been possible without the help of several noteworthy individuals whom I would like to thank here:

Gus Sauter, an enormously talented graphic artist, is the person responsible for the layout, artwork and a great portion of the new photography. Paul Votano, Marketing Director of the cemetery and an author in his own right, was tremendously patient in helping to guide me throughout the process and keeping the project on track. In all probability, the book would never have seen the light of day without the assistance of these two gentlemen.

Mary Ellen Pollina, on the other hand, not only got me started but also encouraged me to make the tome more than just a history book but a work in which my true feelings for the cemetery would emerge.

My son, Ed, was also there at the outset and helped me to keep it going as well.

Malcolm Kriger, Michael Lemish and Mary Elizabeth Thurston all contributed complete chapters which augmented and improved the overall quality and content of the book.

Joe Vericker has for many years been the semi-official photographer of the cemetery and some of his excellent work is exhibited here..

Pat Grosso, my friend and co-director of the cemetery, has been a staunch supporter encouraging me all the way.

Irene Lassen Samar, who preceded our arrival here, supplied some important data and photos for the 1941-1974 period of the cemetery's history.

Of course, none of this would have been conceivable without the effort of the founder himself, Dr. Samuel K. Johnson, and attorneys Gustavus W. Rawson, Arthur S. Lauria and Charles Bates Dana, who in 1913 consented to act as a committee for the express purpose of protecting the interests of those holding plots in the cemetery then, now and in the future.

And last, but far from least, my wife, Ginny, has helped me in more ways than I can ever count in this endeavor and all others.

Edward C. Martin, Jr., Bronxville, New York, September 24, 1997

Contents

©1997 Hartsdale Canine Cemetery, Inc.
All Rights Reserved
Published 1997
Printed in the United States of America
by Image Graphics Inc. Paducah, KY
Library of Congress Catalog Number: 97-94420
ISBN: 0-9659266-0-5

Every effort has been made to ensure the accuracy of the information herein.
However, the authors and Hartsdale Canine Cemetery, Inc. are not responsible for any errors or
omissions that may have occurred.

Introduction

The story of the Hartsdale Canine Cemetery is a celebration of life. It is about the lives of over 100,000 pets and the people who loved them. People from every station of life. Some are very famous, in theater, literature or sports, and their contributions are known to millions around the world. Some are very rich, princesses of faraway kingdoms, patrons of the arts and scions of business. More often, they are like you and me, ordinary people who have loved and lost a good friend.

Over the past twenty years, it has been my privilege to meet thousands of these people and share in their intimate moments of sorrow. Several of them are etched in my memory forever. Their stories are part of the tapestry of the cemetery's history and some of their stories will appear in the pages of this book.

My family's association with the Hartsdale Canine Cemetery spans five generations. At about the same time the first pet was interred at Hartsdale, my great grandfather and his cousin, Robert Caterson, were the proprietors of a successful monument business outside of Woodlawn Cemetery in the Bronx, New York. Robert Caterson was a renowned designer and sculptor who had worked on many distinguished buildings, including Grand Central Station in New York City. In 1918, he was chosen by the Hartsdale Canine Cemetery to design the War Dog Memorial in honor of the canine heroes of World War I.

What is today St. Andrew's Episcopal Church was once part of the historic Phillipse Estate.

During the 1930s my father joined the Caterson family monument business which had since relocated to Valhalla, New York, less than five miles north of Hartsdale. Meanwhile, the landscape of the Hartsdale Canine Cemetery was changing dramatically. Formerly an indulgence of the very rich, dignified burials for devoted pets were now available to people from all walks of life. And, as World War II drew to a close, the marble and granite used for monuments became more readily available. Hartsdale, as well as several other local cemeteries, now displayed samples of available headstones to their plot-holders. My dad had developed a reputation as a master engraver and was sought after for both his craftsmanship and his artistry. In the late 1940s, the owners of the Hartsdale Canine Cemetery entered into an exclusive arrangement with my father to engrave their headstones.

My first memory of the Hartsdale Canine Cemetery occurred shortly after my father began his work there. One day when I was about ten years old, I had the unsettling sense that my mother was quite upset about something. As soon as my father walked through the door, she erupted into tears. "Eddie," she sobbed, "don't ever leave this around the house again. I've been crying all day." In her hands she held the tracing paper that was used to engrave a headstone. The inscription read: "To my best little boy: 1938-1947." My father smiled and embraced his wife. "Bertha, honey, this monument is for a dog." My mother was surprised, but no less heartbroken. Today, my mother's compassion is the foundation of our service to pet-owners. For almost twenty years she received the sorrowful calls and gently explained our procedures with understanding and sensitivity. Our mail includes hundreds of cards and letters from pet owners who have never forgotten her honest sympathy and respect for their grief.

Despite my lineage of stonecutters, I pursued a career as a certified public accountant. In 1973, I was the father of two young sons, working long hours for a public accounting firm and attending graduate school at night. The Hartsdale Canine Cemetery was now owned by Irene Lassen. Mrs. Lassen's husband had died, and she confided to my father that she would like to retire. They wanted to find someone who would both continue the tradition of excellence and understand the financial complexities of the business. My father suggested that the Lassens speak to me. I knew that the cemetery was maintained with impeccable honesty and dignity. Mrs. Lassen was deeply committed to the pet owners and never traded upon their grief. She trusted me to carry on this commitment. I enlisted the help of my childhood friend, Pat Grosso, and together we became the third owners of the Hartsdale Canine Cemetery.

What began as a business venture would soon become a passion, fueled by the thousands of wonderful people who have entrusted me with their beloved pets. Bereaved owners would shyly admit that they were often surprised by the depth of their grief. Here at Hartsdale, they felt kinship with others who had lost a beloved companion. As visitors amble through the gently sloping paths, each monument is tribute to the joy that a pet has brought to someone's life. In sharing their grief, I have discovered the common thread that links the king and the commoner, the rich and the poor, the mighty and the meek. It is the love for a pet, so simple, so pure, so rare and so cherished that is the legacy of the Hartsdale Canine Cemetery.

Dr. Johnson's Apple Orchard

*An Epitaph to a Faithful Companion
Written by Lord Byron*

*"Near this spot lie the remains of
one who possessed beauty without vanity,
strength without insolence, courage
without ferocity, and all the virtues of
man without his vices. This praise,
which would be unmeaning flattery if
inscribed over human ashes, is but a
just tribute to the memory of my loving
and faithful Boatswain – a dog."*

In 1896, the land that is now the Hartsdale Canine Cemetery, and was once part of the Philipse Estate and later the campsite of the Colonial Army during the Battle of White Plains, was an apple orchard owned by Dr. Samuel Johnson, a veterinarian. Besides his private practice, Dr. Johnson was a professor of veterinary surgery at New York Hospital and served as the official veterinarian of the State of New York. He was also a pioneer in the field of animal welfare and one of the founders of the American Society for the Prevention of Cruelty to Animals. Despite the doctor's highly successful career, today he is most remembered for something he never really planned - the first and finest pet cemetery in America.

One day a distressed client of Dr. Johnson's entered his office on West 23rd street in New York with an urgent problem. Her dog had just died and she wanted to give it a proper burial. There was no way for this to be accomplished legally in the City of New York. After considering the problem, the compassionate doctor arrived at a solution. If the woman wanted to make the trip to Hartsdale, he would be pleased to allow her to bury her pet in his apple orchard. The distraught woman gratefully accepted and made the sad journey to the little hamlet in Westchester. While the woman's name has been lost in the mists of time and there are no records of the burial, nor a stone marking the grave's location, we can be certain that her pet is safe somewhere in this peaceful kingdom for no animal has ever been removed from there.

A rural, dirt-road Central Avenue on a lazy summer afternoon in the late 1800s just prior to the genesis of the Hartsdale Pet Cemetery (located on the left).

The Hartsdale train station, which is located a mile from Dr. Johnson's apple orchard, as it must have appeared to the unknown woman who was the cemetery's first client. It is here that pet-owners arrived from New York City.

This burial was not intended to be the beginning of a pet cemetery, but a short time later Dr. Johnson innocently gave impetus to the idea. One day while having lunch with a reporter friend, the doctor casually told the story of the woman's plight and the dog's burial. Within a few days, much to Dr. Johnson's surprise, the story appeared in print. And to his further surprise, he soon found himself the recipient of hundreds of requests from people looking for a place to bury their beloved pets. It was almost as if he had awakened a longing that every pet owner across America had felt - a dignified and protected burial ground for their departed companion.

Before long, Dr. Johnson had set aside a section of the apple orchard to be used as a burial ground for pets. Originally each pet was taken before burial to Dr. Johnson's clinic, documented, placed in a casket and sent to the cemetery. The owners would travel to Hartsdale to attend the burial. Flower arrangements, wire fences and stone markers were used to identify the grave sites. The orchard began to take on the look of a rural cemetery. Soon the markers became larger and funerals more elaborate. In 1899, a spaniel, Major, was buried at the cemetery in a satin-lined casket, complete with a crystal window in the lid. As the flower-draped casket was lowered into the grave, the mourners sang a doxology.

The site of the legendary first burial in Dr. Johnson's apple orchard in 1896.

A rare photo of the esteemed Dr. Samuel Johnson whose simple act of kindness more than one hundred years ago led to the establishment of America's first pet cemetery.

The west gate of the cemetery on what was then Old Road and is now North Washington Avenue.

It didn't take long before word of Dr. Johnson's apple orchard began to spread. An increasing number of people came and began to erect monuments and construct protective iron enclosures.

A section of the cemetery in its earliest days when individual pet-owners took personal care of their pets' resting places as they saw fit.

1896 EVENTS

- *Utah became a state.*
- *The Nobel Prizes were established.*
- *S.P. Langley's flying machine made two successful flights seven years before the Wright Brothers.*
- *Composer Giacamo Puccini introduced his opera, "La Boheme."*
- *First Olympiad of the modern era held in Athens, Greece.*
- *Harriet Beecher Stowe, author of "Uncle Tom's Cabin," died.*
- *William McKinley, running on the gold standard platform, defeated William Jennings Bryan, for the presidency.*
- *America's first pet cemetery was established.*

WHERE TO BURY A DOG

Beneath a cherry tree or an apple tree is an excellent place to bury a dog. Beneath such trees he slept in the drowsy summer. On a hill where the wind is unrebuked, and the trees are roaring, or beside a stream he knew in puppyhood, or somewhere in the flatness of a pasture lane – these are good places in life or in death.

Yet it is a small matter, for if the dog be well remembered, if sometimes he leaps through your dreams, eyes kindling, laughing, begging it matters not at all where that dog sleeps. Nothing is gained – nothing is lost – if memory lives. So, there is really only one place to bury a dog.

If you bury him in this spot, he will come to you when you call – come to you over the grim frontiers of death and down the well – remembered path to your side again. People may scoff at you. Smile at them, for you know something that is hidden from them. The best place to bury a dog is in your heart.

—Taken from a message written by an unknown plot-holder and placed on the cemetery's office wall.

I experienced loss for the first time at the age of eight, when my kitten, Dixie, was accidentally hit and killed by a car. Dixie's death was a terribly painful experience for me because he was my very special friend. When I needed companionship, Dixie and I played together, and when I felt alone or frightened, I petted him and held him close.

Through nuturing and caring for Dixie, I was able to give love, experience, affection and learn responsibilty. Memories of Dixie following me from room to room, kneading my tummy with his paws and licking my neck while he purred endlessly, will be etched in my mind forever.

Life with Dixie was filled with love and companionship. Through his death, I learned the painful realities of life and the consequences of attachment. Looking back on the experience as an adult, I understand that it is as natural to feel loss as it is to feel love.

I was terribly confused when I learned of Dixie's death. I couldn't believe that I wouldn't be playing and cuddling with my best little friend anymore.

Then my parents took me to the pet cemetery to pick out a monument for Dixie. I remember placing the flower in the casket and noticing how peaceful he looked, as though he were sleeping. It was at that moment that the pain which had been in the pit of my stomach for days finally disappeared. Somehow, knowing he was in a safe and peaceful place helped me say goodbye to him and move on.

—Reflection by Carolyn.

Many of the early gravesites
included monuments and
ornate lot enclosures which
were reminiscent of classic
Victorian-style cemeteries.

By 1905, Dr. Johnson's orchard had gained enough recognition to be written about in The New York Times. On September 3rd of that year a featured story appeared under the headline "A Canine Cemetery of Three Acres in Which Scores of Pets are Interred - Hundreds of Dollars Spent on Graves and Grave Stones by Their Sorrowing Owners." The article spoke of dogs being "...laid away with deepest regret and strong affection." It also reported that while the cemetery had started with the burial of dogs, it was actually opened to cats and other animals. In fact, one of the most elaborate plots at the time was a showpiece for a cat named Mignon. It had boxed shrubs, two flower gardens and a private caretaker who moonlighted from his

regular job at Woodlawn Cemetery in the Bronx, New York. The man was paid to make sure that the grass was always kept cropped, the shrubbery trimmed and the flowers in bloom.

Though hundreds of interments had been made by 1913, the rights associated with those who had made interments were very uncertain. In the spring of that year a committee headed by three prominent attorneys, Arthur S. Lauria, Charles Bates Dana and Gustavus W. Rawson, was formed for the purpose of protecting the interests of plot-holders and receiving voluntary contributions to improve the cemetery.

On April 21, 1914, the cemetery was incorporated in order to take the necessary measures to ensure that the land would always be utilized as a pet cemetery.

Mignon, a cat, was honored by her family with an elaborate plot surrounded by boxed shrubs and two flower gardens. A private caretaker worked part-time when he finished work at the human Woodlawn Cemetery in New York to tend this unique showplace.

The Early Years

*The only sorrow you ever brought me
was the day you left.*

Taken from a monument at the Hartsdale Pet Cemetery.

Through the generous contributions of plot-holders the land began to resemble the look of a human cemetery. Additional tracts of land were acquired. An iron fence was erected around the entire grounds, new paths installed and scores of trees planted. A full-time caretaker was hired and a cottage (the present office) was built. Trust funds were established to ensure the continuation of the cemetery.

In the 1920s as the cemetery continued to improve and expand, people from everywhere - including many celebrities - were burying their pets at Hartsdale in greater numbers.

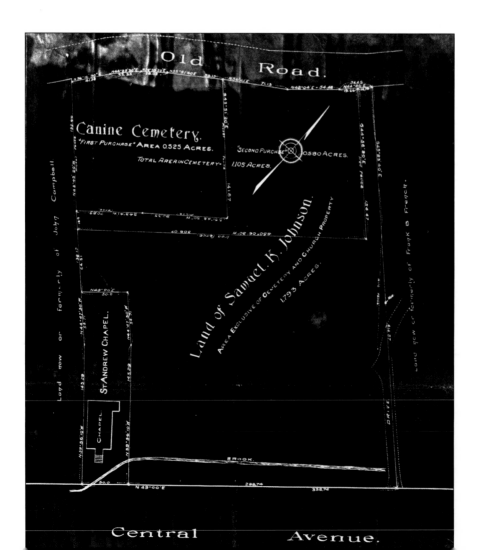

After the cemetery was officially incorporated, a full-time care-taker was contracted to be on the grounds and a cottage was built for his needs.

The path leading to the care-taker's home is now the office and receiving area for those who bring their pets to Hartsdale. It is here that their burial preferences are arranged.

The original classic wrought iron gate served as a stunning entrance for visitors in the early years.

Erected in the early 1900s, the Walsh Memorial is believed to be the first above-ground pet mausoleum.

Elaborate funerals and expensive monuments were not uncommon in this period. In 1915, Mrs. M.F. Walsh arranged at an estimated cost of twenty-five thousand dollars for the construction of the cemetery's first mausoleum. Made of the finest Barre granite and weighing in excess of fifty tons, it is still the largest and most expensive monument ever erected at the cemetery. It is said Mrs. Walsh supervised every aspect of the construction. Five Walsh pets are now interred here.

In 1918, shortly after World War I, a move to honor all dogs that had served in the war began at Hartsdale. Contributions from plot-holders and the general public were used to erect a majestic ten-foot high monument which is topped with a bronze statue of a shepherd dog. The following inscription is etched in the monument:

"Dedicated to the memory of the war dog. Erected by public contribution by dog lovers to man's faithful friend for the valiant services rendered in the World War, 1914 - 1918."

The monument serves as the focal point of a ceremony held at the cemetery every Memorial Day to honor canines who have performed extraordinary feats of courage. American Legion Post 8 in nearby New Rochelle announced that the custom of placing a wreath at the memorial would be continued by a special resolution in the bylaws of the post.

The renowned War Dog Memorial was constructed in 1923 and is believed to be the first of its kind.

DEDICATED
TO THE MEMORY OF
THE WAR DOG
ERECTED BY PUBLIC CONTRIBUTION
BY DOG LOVERS, TO MAN'S MOST
FAITHFUL FRIEND, FOR THE VALIANT
SERVICES RENDERED IN THE
WORLD WAR
1914 — 1918

The first expansion of the cemetery included the installation of new paths and the planting of trees (circa 1922).

Over the years, many pets have shared their lifetime with me.

Each one has left a lasting memory...

My first pet was a small green parakeet, who repeated not only his name (Chico, Chico, Pretty Boy Chico) over and over, but also copied our calling of my independent black and white tomcat, (Tommy, Tommy, Tommy). They lived together, along with my brother's tropical fish collection, and a family dog named Smokey.

Smokey, a black lab mix seemed to smile when overcome with joy and delight by our return at the end of the day. He thought that Tommy was his playmate, much to the cat's dismay. But Tommy always had the upper hand, even though Smokey was four times his size.

Many years later, as an adult with my own family, a very special animal came to live with us. Although abandoned on the side of a parkway, undernourished, with tangled hair, she was the most gentle and loving golden English Cocker Spaniel: our very beautiful Ophelia.

From the beginning, she was totally devoted to me — even leaving her new born pups, so she could sleep by my side, as she did each night, until in her later years stairs became impossible for her to mount. When we discovered that she was pregnant, we couldn't part with all her

"babies." We couldn't break her heart. So we kept one of her daughters, Mona, to live with us, and sent her other pups to live among family members.

Ophie took such loving care of Mona, cleaning her face and teaching her the art of gentleness and devotion. Although she became blind at a young age, she always knew where to find me and was content just to lay nearby and wait for a kind word or a soft pat on her beautiful head. She fended off our last son's early years of curiosity by licking his face over and over until, finally, he would crawl away and leave her in peace. Never a growl, never a nip...Ophelia died very suddenly, early one morning. Her death was unexpected, without warning, and we were overcome with grief, for she was more than just our family pet, she was a very loving and faithful friend. Ophie will always be cherished in our memories. She was laid to rest among other family members' beloved pets in Dr. Johnson's Apple Orchard.

But Ophie had left us a wonderful gift in her gentle, shy pup, Mona, who helped to fill the void left by her mother. Monie lived with us for 17 years, until she too passed on and joined her mother, sisters and brother at Hartsdale. There she lies peacefully among her family.

The pain of separating from each of these beautiful

View of the same section of the cemetery as it appears today.

pets was so very difficult and just when I decided – enough – no more pets… Coach entered my life.

A most protective German Shepherd mix of a dog – who came to our family from a local shelter, via a young man who was a basketball coach, and thus he was named. Coach works so very hard at protecting our family that it's very hard to get annoyed at his loud barks of warning and announcement of his presence in our home to all who pass by.

He grows dearer to me each year with his complete devotion and faithfulness to our son Brian and me. When Brian is sleeping, if anyone heads toward his room, Coach dashes ahead on alert and jumps on the bed to place his body over Brian's to protect him with his life, while Brian sleeps. Coach is enjoyed and loved by us all

The unconditional love and devotion that an animal gives, so freely, without expecting anything in return, is the glorious gift they offer us. All of my pets have enriched my life by their unrestrained friendship. I shall always remember each pet, each spirit remains within my heart. Each pet had a separate identity and personality that made then endearing and lovable, and because of them my life has been greatly enhanced.

—Reflection by Ginny

The monuments ranged from the very simple to the very elaborate. These panoramic landscape shots depict the rural apple orchard being developed into a pet cemetery at the turn-of the-century.

The rural cemetery began to take on the look of a well-manicured human cemetery, (circa 1920).

After learning that the Waldorf Astoria in New York would not allow her pets to stay with her, arrangements were made for her and her party, including her pets, to stay at the Plaza Hotel. The Plaza must have suited the princess well for she stayed there for five years.

Upon a visit to Ringling Brothers Circus, the princess fell in love with a young lion cub and tried to buy him from the Ringlings. After a lengthy transaction with the circus, she acquired the cub and brought him home by limousine to live with her at the Plaza. Princess Parlaghy officially christened the lion "General Sickles" in honor of a civil war hero whose portrait she had painted. However, she called him Goldfleck. Sadly, as the cub was growing into a full-size lion he grew ill and died. After a formal wake at the Plaza, Goldfleck was taken by the princess to Hartsdale for burial in 1912.

In the early part of this century Irene Castle and her husband, Vernon, were America's most renowned dance team. Besides being a superb dancer and an international symbol of youth and beauty, Irene Castle was an ardent lover of animals. She used her fame and fortune to help them. The famous Orphans of the Storm Animal Shelter near Chicago was founded by her in 1928. Irene Castle, dancer and humanitarian, buried five dogs and a monkey at Hartsdale.

Among the international celebrities who started coming to the cemetery in the 20s was Irene Castle, who with her husband, Vernon, headlined all over the world as a renowned dance team. They were the fashion setters of the day but Irene Castle preferred to be known as an animal lover. Here she is pictured with her pet monkey, "Rastus". He is buried with her other pets at Hartsdale and, after his death, she wrote a tribute placed on the office wall, which read:

"Rastas, the smartest most lovable monkey that ever lived".

In the 1920s Christine Norman, a Broadway actress, was considered one of the most beautiful women in the world. She starred in the Broadway production of "Peg O' My Heart." It seemed that she had everything: beauty, talent, money and fame. However, a few years after she buried her pet Japanese terrier, Sandy, at Hartsdale, she leaped to her death from the twentieth floor of a New York City hotel.

When her mother learned that Christine's will called for a certain amount of money be put aside for the upkeep of her pet's grave, she took the matter to court. She filed suit to overthrow the will, claiming her daughter was "obviously of unsound mind and the victim of fraud and undue influence."

Actress Christine Norman was a Broadway "superstar" many decades ago and, as were so many of the celebrities who came to Hartsdale, she was an avid pet lover. In this rare photograph, she is shown with her dog, Sandy, who is buried in Dr. Johnson's apple orchard. The scene is from the 1920s hit, "Peg O' My Heart."

A Tribute to Man's Best Friend
Eulogy to a Dog
By Senator George Graham Vest

Gentlemen of the jury. The best friend a man has in this world may turn against him and become his enemy. His son and daughter that he has reared with loving care may become ungrateful. Those who are nearest and dearest to us, those whom we trust with our happiness and our good name, may become traitors to their faith. The money that a man has he may lose. It flies away from him when he may need it most. Man's reputation may be sacrificed in a moment of ill-considered action. The people who are prone to fall on their knees and do us honor when success is with us may be the first to throw the stone of malice when failure settles its cloud upon our heads. The one absolutely unselfish friend a man may have in this selfish world, the one that never deserts him, the one that never proves ungrateful or treacherous, is the dog.

Gentlemen of the jury, a man's dog stands by him in prosperity and poverty, in health and in sickness. He will sleep on the cold ground when the wintry winds blow and the snow drives fiercely, if only he may be near this master's side. He will kiss the hand that has no food to offer, he will lick the wounds and sores that come in encounter with the roughness of the world. He guards the sleep of his pauper master as if he were a prince.

When all other friends desert, he remains. When riches take wings and reputation falls to pieces, he is as constant in his love as the sun in its journey through the heavens. If fortune drives the master forth an outcast into the world, friendless and homeless, the faithful dog asks no higher privilege than that of accompanying him, to guard him against danger, to fight against his enemies, and when the last scene of all comes, and death takes his master in its embrace and his body is laid in the cold ground, no matter if all other friends pursue their way, there by his graveside will the noble dog be found, his head between his paws and his eyes sad, but open, in alert watchfulness and true, even unto death. ◆

More than seventy-five years ago, Mrs. Cornelia Polhemus Meserole had a monument erected to her beloved dogs and specified in her will that ten thousand dollars be given to the Hartsdale Cemetery for the repair and preservation of her loving tribute. Interestingly, Mrs. Meserole and others who have left similar instructions recall the trials and tribulations of Christine Norman. But times had changed and there were no sensational court battles. These wishes were carried out without fanfare except for human interest stories in several newspapers.

However, Arthur Garfield Hays, well-known lawyer and civil libertarian, maintained that Christine's will merely reflected the thoughts and concerns of a caring, loving woman of integrity. The court agreed and ruled the will invalid. Christine's terrier at Hartsdale had won. The actress' wishes were respected and carried out.

Apparently the legal precedent set in the lawsuit over Christine Norman's will inspired others to do the same. Marion C. Robinson directed her executors to scatter her ashes over the grave of her German shepherd Chief's grave, and to pay a sum of money to Hartsdale for the perpetual care for Chief's resting place. Mrs. Cornelia Polhemus Meserole left ten thousand dollars for the repair and preservation of a monument to her dogs that were buried at Hartsdale in 1914.

James S. Sherman, vice president of the United States from 1908 until 1912, and Jimmy Walker, the mayor of the city of New York, also interred their pets in the cemetery in this era.

In the 1920s, Hartsdale was known as the place where the very rich and very famous buried their pets. Large and elaborate monuments marked the graves of pampered pets. All seemed well at America's first pet cemetery.

"Chief's" mistress chose to have her cremated remains scattered over her pet's grave.

A Time for Change

He came into my life
for want of a meal and a place to stay…
He left with my heart.
Taken from a monument in the Hartsdale Pet Cemetery.

The Great Depression of the 1930s affected much of the United States and the cemetery was no exception. Income from the trust funds established in an earlier period enabled the cemetery to survive. Dr. Johnson died in 1937 and his estate took control of the corporation. Clearly, the time to seek new leadership had come. As America was about to enter the second world war, the era of Dr. Johnson came to an end.

Chris Scheu lived across the street from the cemetery and would often amble through the peaceful apple orchard after work. During these visits, he often chatted with the caretaker who informed him that the cemetery was pursuing a new direction. Having grown up on a farm, he felt passionately about animals and saw this as an opportunity to do something which greatly interested him. In addition, like most residents of the small rural suburb, he was proud of the pet cemetery and well aware of its history. As a young man, he had witnessed some of the elaborate funerals held at the famous cemetery. When his friend and business associate, C. George Lassen agreed to help him, the challenge of restoring the cemetery to its original beauty began. On December 31, 1941, with some trepidation, the two young men assumed responsibility of the cemetery.

This simple but quaint cottage served as Dr. Johnson's summer retreat. Here he enjoyed peace and solace from the fast-paced climate of New York City. The cottage today (at left) houses the cemetery's administrative offices.

Dedicated pet owners willingly contributed funds to enhance the beauty of the grounds. A fence was erected to surround the area, an entrance way constructed and a large selection of graceful trees planted.

The west gate of the cemetery as it appears today.

ignificant changes took place over the next few years as the cemetery was operated with a more "hands-on" approach. In 1942, the office in New York City was closed and all records were transferred to Hartsdale. George Lassen and his wife, Irene, moved into the original vacation home of Dr. Johnson on the cemetery grounds. The two men, aided by their families, worked long hours every day. The fruits of their labor began to show as the cemetery was returned to the graceful place it had been a decade before.

As in the past, Hartsdale continued to be a place where many well-known personalities buried their pets. Celebrities such as Xavier Cugat, Kate Smith, Robert Merrill, Fritz Kreisler, Elizabeth Arden, Hetty Green, Dagmar, Gloria DeHaven, Barry Gray, George Raft and Gene Krupa buried pets during this period. And, with the Great Depression now in the past and the concept of pet burial gaining wider social acceptance as a result of canines displaying never-before-seen bravery and valor in combat, many middle-class Americans were also bringing their pets to the famous cemetery. In addition, the cemetery was now "family" operated. Rigid rules and regulations were eliminated. More families now felt comfortable with the new owners.

*Following the harsh days of the Depression, the hard work of George Lassen and
Chris Scheu restored the cemetery to its former graceful appearance.*

Christian Scheu, co-director from 1941 until 1963, loved the cemetery as a child in Hartsdale, and continued to visit when he was in his late nineties.

Chris Scheu tells of a couple who arrived at the cemetery one evening as the gates were being closed. Thinking that the couple were visitors, he asked them to come back the next day. The couple explained that their dog had died and they traveled a long way to bury him at Harstdale. Chris, remembering the compassion of Dr. Johnson toward the unknown woman who buried her pet in his apple orchard, kept the cemetery open and arranged for the burial immediately.

During the 1950s, Irene Lassen recalls speaking with a couple who visited the cemetery frequently and always placed fresh flowers on the pet's plot. They told Mrs. Lassen their son had been killed in the Korean War and his body was unable to be returned to this country. They told Mrs. Lassen that his dog's grave allowed them to feel closer to their son.

C. George Lassen, co-director of the cemetery after Dr. Johnson's death, moved with his family to the cemetery, making it the first time someone was on the premises day and night.

Irene Lassen, who managed the cemetery with dignity and excellence until 1974, pictured with her son, Ray.

MACPHERSON

JACK
1877–1962

PEGGY
1875–1949

AND
THEIR BELOVED PETS

During their tenure, the Lassens found a small, stray terrier-beagle mix puppy who was wandering through the neighborhood. Without hesitation they decided to make her part of their family and named her Susie. Susie seemed to realize that she lived in a special place and that the people with whom she came into contact had special needs. Soon she became the queen of the Hartsdale Canine Cemetery. She greeted visitors and was always on hand to share their grief and offer solace. The cemetery was always her domain, and in a way it still is. Susie now rests here beside the main walk at the back gate.

When George Lassen died in 1961 and Chris Scheu retired soon after, the cemetery was operated by George Lassen's widow, Irene, until 1974. It was the end of another era.

Buried in Mrs. Cheever-Poster's plot are eight Irish Setters – all champions.

The Lassen family dog, Susie, lived at the cemetery for fourteen years. Through her intuition she comforted the grieving by leading the procession, bowing her head in prayer and giving a mournful howl. She was beloved by plot owners throughout the world.

Andy Samar, husband of Irene Lassen Samar, served as operations manager of the cemetery in the early 1970s.

Boots, a moviestar dog, once earned three thousand dollars a week. During World War II, he was responsible for selling nine million dollars worth of war bonds, and appeared at a command performance for President Franklin D. Roosevelt. When Boots was buried at Hartsdale at the age of sixteen, his funeral was attended by Hollywood friends and fans. He had appeared in more than a dozen pictures, and was awarded an Oscar for his performance in "Emergency Squad".

After devoting 33 years to "The Peaceable Kingdom," Irene Lassen was ready to pass the keys to a new generation. Mrs. Lassen's love for Hartsdale ran very deep, and she wanted to be sure that her successors would not only share their love for animals but were also astute in business matters that the changing times demanded. She sought advice from monument designer, plot-holder and friend, Edward Caterson Martin, who she had come to know over the last twenty years as a master craftsman of some of Hartsdale's most beautiful monuments. It was Martin's cousin, Robert Caterson, who designed and built the famous War Dog Memorial.

Mr. Martin suggested that she talk to his son, Ed Jr., a practicing Certified Public Accountant, about managing the cemetery so that she could retire. Like Christian Scheu did thirty five years earlier, Edward C. Martin, Jr., asked a long-time friend to join him. On April 17, 1974, responsibility for the cemetery was transferred to Edward Martin and Patrick Grosso.

Edward C. Martin, Sr., master engraver, spent most of his working life creating magnificent monuments that still make America's first pet cemetery a showplace of ultimate artistic expression. For more than forty years, he crafted his masterworks at his studio just a few miles from Hartsdale.

Ed Martin, Jr.

Pat Grosso

Bertha Martin

Directors, Patrick A. Grosso and Edward C. Martin, Jr., have deep personal feelings for this special place. Both have pets buried here, and have been involved with the cemetery since 1974.

The Hartsdale Pet Cemetery as it appeared to the new directors, Edward C. Martin, Jr. and Patrick A. Grosso, on April 17, 1974.

Continuing the Tradition

Personal Reflection

*The apple trees were just beginning to bloom
in the spring of 1974 when Pat and I began our tenure
as the new owners of the cemetery. Even though
I had often visited the tiny wooden cottage that served as
the cemetery's office, it was as though I was seeing
it for the first time. The knotty pine walls were covered
with literally hundreds of photographs, messages,
cards and poems from bereaved owners who wanted to
share memories of their departed pets with others.
The Lassens and Scheus had faithfully honored every
request. At that moment the full impact of this
responsibility descended on me. I felt at once the
enormous commitment to the thousands of pets buried
at Hartsdale as well as to the loving and compassionate
people who entrusted me with their beloved animals.
The season of renewal that ushered in our first days here
would always remind me that more than anything else,
Hartsdale is a celebration of life.*

"The Peaceable Kingdom" is a private refuge for pet owners who visit and reflect on times past with a beloved companion. Everyday many come, even years later, to express their enduring love.

Directors Pat Grosso and Ed Martin at the cemetery's Centennial Celebration on September 29, 1996.

P at and I shared the same vision as George Lassen, Chris Scheu and Dr. Johnson – to allow pet owners to bury their pets in a place that was as dignified and beautiful as the finest human cemeteries. I recall Mrs. Lassen's words of advice: "Remember, those who choose to bury their pets, do so because they want to, not because they have to." The myths I had heard were not true. Those who bury their pet animals do not care more about animals than humans – they are simply caring people who think this is the right thing to do. While celebrities such as Joe Garagiola, Ralph Kiner and Diana Ross brought their pets to Hartsdale during my tenure here, there were far more ordinary people from all walks of life who also buried their pets.

My memory is filled with thoughts of the people who buried their pets at Hartsdale: of Raymond Snyder who paid for the burial of pets owned by individuals he never met, of Elio Lithgow who visited the cemetery every weekend until he became too ill to do so, of Malcolm Kriger whose love for pets and Hartsdale motivated him to write the book, "The Peaceable Kingdom in Hartsdale;" and of the policeman who fought off tears when his canine partner who had saved his life was brought to Hartsdale.

And then there was the blind newsdealer from the courthouse in New Rochelle, Mr. Groom, whose burial of his seeing-eye dog, Tim, drew over a hundred people from clerks to judges. Or Mrs. Jean Claire McCall Josephson who came all the way from Maine to bury her pet because no other pet cemetery in her immediate vicinity would do.

I was also pleasantly surprised at one point to come in contact with two of my teachers from high school, Miss Roget and Mr. Nicou, who had also come to Hartsdale to bury their pets. In addition, a colleague of mine at Iona College, Tom Pollina, chose Hartsdale as the final resting place for his pet, Atticus. And I could never forget Chickie, the Puerto Rican native from the Bronx who composed her own final tribute to her beloved pets in as touching and moving a manner as one would ever find in a classic book of poetry:

Prayer at the death of Virgo (13) and Tweety (13)

Lord God,
to those who have never had a pet,
this prayer will sound strange,
but to You, Lord of All Life and
Creator of All Creatures,
it will be understandable.
My heart is heavy
as I face the loss in death of
my beloved Virgo & Tweety
who were so much a part of my life.

Virgo & Tweety made my life more enjoyable
and gave me cause to laugh
and to find joy in their company.
I remember the fidelity and loyalty
of Virgo & Tweety
and will miss them being with me.
From them I learned many lessons,
such as quality of naturalness and
the unembarrassed request for affection.
In caring for their daily needs,
I was taken up and out of my own self-needs
and thus learned to service another.

May the death of Virgo & Tweety
remind me that death comes to all of us,
animal and human,
and that it is the natural passage for all life.
May Virgo & Tweety sleep on
in eternal slumber in Your Godly care as all
creation awaits the fullness of liberation.

Amen

Police Dog Burial; 1996 Memorial Day

I am convinced that despite differences in religion, race, finances and social status, those who choose to bury their pet have one thing in common – they are thoughtful people of integrity who have lost a good friend. A friend who did not ask what school they went to or what they did for a living. A friend who did not care what they looked like or what kind of car they drove. A friend who was so loyal that he would sacrifice his life to protect his master. They come to Dr. Johnson'd apple orchard seeking a means to honor the memory of their pet. We try to help keep that memory alive.

Apple trees planted in 1996 during the Centennial Celebration symbolize the rebirth of the original orchard.

The monument, which is the centerpiece of the Memorial Flower Garden, pays tribute to all pets brought to Hartsdale.

Each year during the winter holiday season, the cemetery conducts a tree lighting ceremony adjacent to its front gate. Typically, plot-holders are asked to come and bring offerings of pet food which, in turn, are donated in their names to various animal shelters in the area. In previous years, the cemetery has provided donations of its own to be applied to further the training of seeing-eye dogs as well as having plot-holders bring toys and stuffed animals to be given to children in homeless shelters.

oth Pat and I knew the cemetery would have to change in order to accommodate the increasing needs of pet owners. Previously undeveloped land was made available for burial. A beautiful Victorian house built in 1904 was acquired from our neighbor. New paths and landscaping were added each year. Cremation services were made available in 1986. A memorial garden was created for those who wished to scatter their pet's cremated remains. In the early 1980s almost 90 years of hand-written records were computerized. Special services such as the Pet Memorial Day became annual events. In 1991, we were invited to Albany to help formulate policy that would be used to establish legislation regulating pet cemeteries in New York State.

Never forgotten, the hero canines of war are honored every Memorial Day. A tradition that began years ago when a man known only as Arthur came every year to lay a wreath at the War Dog Memorial. For reasons unknown, this veteran of the "Battle of the Bulge" was no longer able to come. In 1981, continuous remembrance was assured when Commander Thaddeus Odgen of American Legion Post 8 in New Rochelle passed a special resolution to the bylaws of his post stating that a wreath, a firing detail and services would be furnished on Memorial Day forever. Hundreds of people now attend these heartfelt services every year.

As the responsibilities of operating the cemetery increased, and as George Lassen and Chris Scheu had done in earlier years, we asked our families for help. Pat's brother, Fran as well as my mother, Bertha, my late uncle, Chester and my brother-in-law, Len, responded and became part of the cemetery. Our sons would join us in later years. Fran's American Eskimo Husky, Brandy, also joined the new team to continue the tradition started by Susie before him. Brandy was the official greeter of the cemetery for 16 years. Now, like Susie, he too rests beside the main walk at the rear gate of the cemetery.

Cemetery foreman, Trevor Gill.

Brandy, Operations Manager Fran Grosso's American Eskimo Husky, succeeded Susie as the cemetery's official greeter.

Cemetery administrator, Len Saccardo.

Ed Martin's late uncle, Chester Reynolds

Into the 21st Century and Beyond

*From the time of the pyramids
to the present day, the frozen pole
to the torrid zone, wherever man has been,
there has been his dog.*

Excerpted from the Hartsdale Canine Cemetery's first brochure (1913)

Human values have changed dramatically in the past one hundred years. However, the relationship that people have with their pets remains the same today as it was in 1896. It is my hope that Dr. Johnson's compassionate act will continue to serve as the cornerstone for pet burials.

As we approach a new millennium, the cemetery must be in a position to meet the challenges that lie ahead. A foundation should be established for the purpose of enhancing the beauty of the cemetery. A wildlife preservation is being planned. Two acres of newly acquired land will be developed. While Hartsdale has always permitted human cremated remains to be buried in their pets' plots, a new section will be dedicated specifically for this purpose. The War Dog Memorial has received much attention, and we feel the time has come to seek national recognition for this historical monument. Finally, with the dawn of the information superhighway upon us, America's first pet cemetery is in the unique position of being accessible to the entire world. Therefore, we have developed a home page on the Internet which will allow pet owners far and wide to visit our historical grounds via cyberspace.

This section of the cemetery was the latest to be developed.

"Dr. Johnson's Apple Orchard"
in the 21st century
as envisioned by the directors.

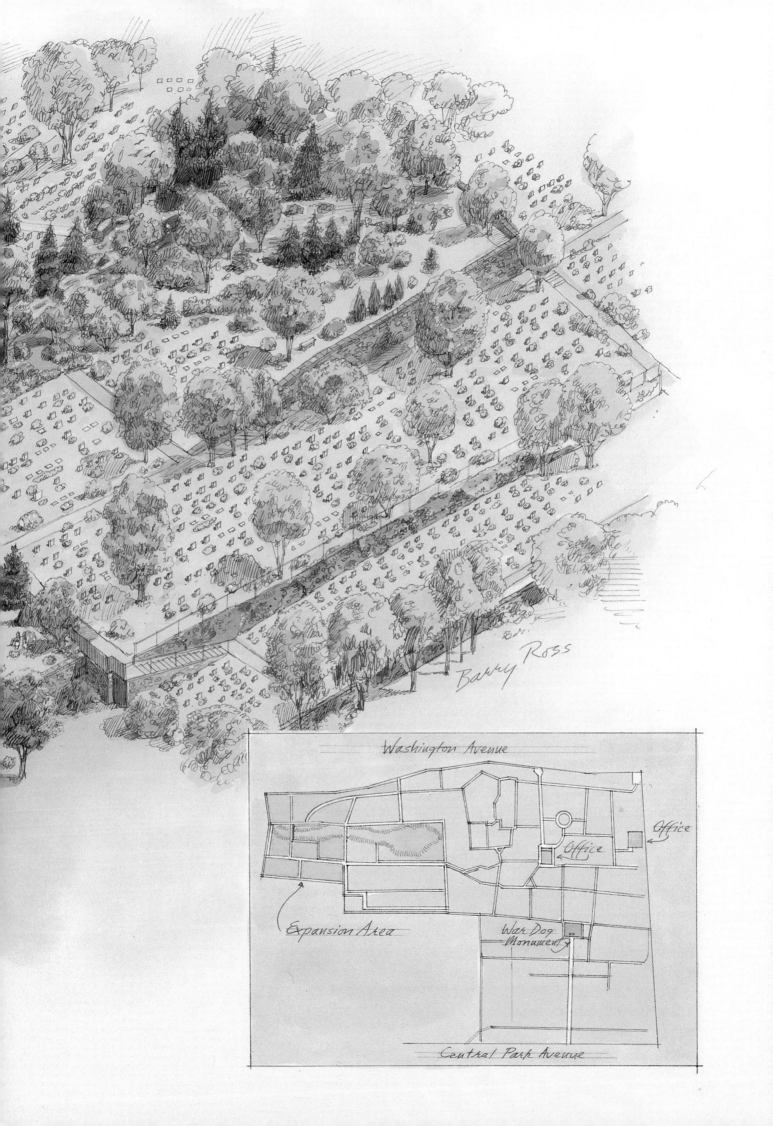

Barry Ross

Washington Avenue

Office

Office

Expansion Area

War Dog Monument

Central Park Avenue

Memoir by Malcom D. Kriger, Author of
The Peaceable Kingdom In Hartsdale

Personal Reflection

*I was 8 years old when my goldfish died.
I went to feed him. He was floating on top of the water.
I ran for some salt because I had been told that salt
revives goldfish. It didn't help, and I knew I had lost
a friend. I also faced death for the first time.
I knew what I wanted to do. Later that morning,
I took him to the backyard and buried him,
using a stick from a popscicle to mark the spot.
Almost fifty years later, I still find satisfaction knowing
that somewhere at my childhood home my goldfish is
part of the earth–and remembered.*

Many years later, after college, I moved to New York, and Wickets, my first dog, came into my life; a six-month old Cairn Terrier who needed a place to live. I took her sight unseen, and she was my dearest friend through 15 years of many struggles in the "big city."

I used to promise her a silver collar from Tiffany's when things got better. She couldn't have cared less. She was happy to share life, and she brought me comfort and happiness through some hard times.

It is with gratitude to Wickets that I eventually wrote "The Peaceable Kingdom in Hartsdale."

Years later, when Wickets decided her time here was at an end all of my heroic efforts to keep her were of no use. She left for the unknown, but in truth she has never left me.

My overwhelming sadness on our journey to that enchanted land was mixed with fear. How would I, with little money, give her the care and respect she deserved? What would happen after I left her there? Would she always have a safe and special place among us?

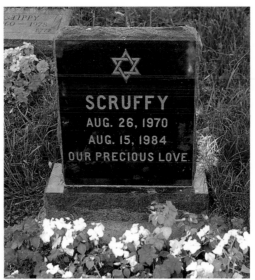

The myth that animals have no souls has been put to rest at Hartsdale. Religious themes are pervasive throughout the historic park.

A pet is not forever, but its loving memory is.

My grief was deep, but my fears were soon gone. For I, like those before and after me, was treated with deep understanding and sympathy. Position in life—wealthy, poor, young or old—was not a consideration. I learned that the time-honored traditions at Hartsdale are as deeply engraved in the cemetery's philosophy as the ageless messages of love in the small head stones and monuments. Wickets was welcomed with open arms as she left mine for the last time.

I visited Wickets several times that spring and summer, and each time I felt better knowing that she was secure. I later discovered that no pet has ever been removed from Hartsdale, even when the original owners were long gone.

But I wanted to know more about the place I had left Wickets, and I decided I would write a book. The year was 1969. It took me 14 years while I worked in a full-time job, did research and saved the money to publish the book exactly the way I wanted it to be.

I knew the title from the beginning. For Hartsdale reminded me of a favorite painting of mine, The Peaceable Kingdom by the early nineteenth century primitive painter Edward Hicks. The original is in the Metropolitan Museum of Art in New York City.

Hicks based this work on Isaiah XI in the Bible, which speaks of such animals as a "wolf…lamb…leopard…lion…kid…calf…sharing the green grass where they lay." Hicks' vision is a world of love and peace, a world that is fully realized in the pet cemetery at Hartsdale.

I spoke to and wrote to more than a thousand men, women and children for my book. I don't believe you could meet a more decent cross-section of people anywhere. These were not animal "nuts" or lonely "kooks," as many detractors would have you believe, but fine human beings who reached out beyond their love of their pets to people in need, to involvement in social issues, to close friends and loving children and grandchildren.

I interviewed those who had made the trip to Hartsdale more than half a century ago; those who had come either a few years ago or just months before. Their memories were fresh; the joys of their loving pets had not diminished; and all felt at peace knowing that their loved ones were under the watchful care of the people at Hartsdale. A common thread was that they felt the cemetery was a lasting celebration of life.

During the years of research and writing "The Peaceable Kingdom in Hartsdale," I wandered through every part of the cemetery, and I still do from time to time.

THOR

1959 — 1967

THERE IS AN OLD BE
THAT ON SOME SOLEMN
BEYOND THE SPHERE O
OLD FRIENDS SHALL MEE

MR. & MRS. DON O

TEDDY SPERRY

A FAITHFUL FRIEND
AND COMPANION
FOR 23 YEARS

Hartsdale Pet Cemetery is a multicultural haven. The common sentiments of love, companionship and loss are themes that cross all barriers as demonstrated by inscriptions written in foreign languages.

Everytime I wander through "The Peaceable Kingdom" I feel a sense of renewal; a confirmation of how caring so many people can be; and, above all, the significance our pets continue to be in our lives. I also feel a sense of calm, knowing that my dogs will always "live" in an atmosphere of love and respect. Never truly gone. Never forgotten.

Etched in thousands of stones, whether a name or a long poem, we know that these were lives well spent, and most worthy of recognition. Poignant, inspiring, sometimes amusing, the messages present a microcosm of the world, an ideal place where race, religion, origin of birth and position in life are accorded equal dignity.

As I roam, I am witness to a century of history, changing attitudes, affirmation of religious belief and statements of pure love.

I am always drawn to one monument in particular. For it sums up the most prevalent wish expressed by those who have made the journey to "The Peaceable Kingdom." It is the resting place of Thor and the message simply states: *"There is an old belief/ That on some solemn shore/ Beyond the sphere of grief/ Old friends shall meet once more."*

To me every etched monument is special, and the ones I mention here are meant to pay homage to all of the others.

Looking out at "The Peaceable Kingdom" from one of its graceful hills I think of Dr. Johnson and the one pet he gave a home to in his apple orchard in 1896. How remarkable it is! For thousands of monuments now grace the land. How rewarding to see it today, a celebrated New York landmark and international gathering for more than 60,000 pets from all over the world.

I discover as I wander that others know, as I know, what "love at first sight" is. For whoever took a pet home without feeling the instant pleasure of mutual love? It may surprise some that many of "The Peaceable Kingdom's" pets were very, very young. Tinkerbelle and Hanky Panky are among the youngest pets here, and even though they were less than a year old, they were lovingly brought to Hartsdale. This reverence for life says a lot to me. For it recognizes love not measured by time, but depth.

Not far away is the opposite extreme. On a twenty-square foot plot, a monument records the name Terry Sperry, a parrot who "was my constant companion for forty years."

Two other monuments that come into my view often hold a place in "The Peaceable Kingdom" book of records.

Pets with high I.Q.s are often named after philosophers and authors.

The oldest monument in the nation's first pet cemetery was erected for "Dotty".

One of the most unique tributes to a pet is a 1929 LeMans Cup from the internationally-famous French automobile race. This prestigious trophy marks the resting place of Black Brook Vin, an aristocratic poodle.

The year 1899 is etched on the cemetery's oldest monument. Now I realize I'm stretching a point, but it intrigues me that this stone will soon be here for a part of three centuries–the 19th, 20th, and in the year 2000, the 21st. This age-old monument is to "Dotty, beloved pet of E.M. Dodge, who Died in Her Fourteenth Year."

Another record holder is the tallest monument. Towering six-feet, it speaks of "Our Loved One Grumpy, August 4, 1913 to September 20, 1926. His sympathetic love and understanding enriched out lives. He waits for us."

"The Peaceable Kingdom" is also the land that includes a gallery of fine sculpture. Throughout the landscape, at practically every turn, I am greeted by distinctive statues of everything from angels, cats, dogs and arches to lambs, deer and even a 1942 stone dog house for Buster. There's a handsome stone bench for Jock; a graceful bas-relief Persian cat named Silver Prince, which has adorned the cemetery for more than seventy years; a modern piece for Doc D'Argon; and a beautiful bird bath embellished with a contented squirrel feeding on an acorn.

One of the most unique tributes to a pet is valuable and historic and, undoubtedly, one of the proudest possessions of those who gave it a place of honor with Black Brook Vinnie. It is the famous Le Mans Cup, sculptured with its magnificent symbol of victory. As prestigious as Hollywood's Oscar or Broadway's Tony award, the Le Mans Cup is still awarded at the internationally famous automobile race at Le Mans, France.

A touching tribute, engraved in brass at the base of this 1929 Le Mans Cup tells that aristocratic Vinnie Boy "clowned, played and loved people as much as any mongrel on earth..." It goes on to recount that Vinnie Boy had a great love for the Bentley Marquee which had won at Le Mans, and that he fell into a peaceful coma in that car while being held by his mistress. The conclusion of the inscription proclaims, "this champion's trophy is his headstone. No other person is more deserving."

As you can see, wandering through "The Peaceable Kingdom" can be full of surprises and drama, and the more I see, the more I realize why this is a place where the world comes together in many, many ways.

To further underscore this, I will tell you about some of the foreign and religious aspects of the cemetery. Considering the many nations, religions, cultures and beliefs found at the cemetery it is evident that this hallowed place is an ideal United Nations where co-existence is a reality.

"The Peaceable Kingdom" is a true "melting pot." I believe an intensive search could possibly find almost every part of the world represented here.

Beloved Egypt probably traveled more than any pet at Hartsdale. According to the inscription, "Beloved Egypt Who Lies Beneath This Stone After A Journey of Thirty Thousand Miles, Weary Traveler Now At Rest Little Traveler God Knew Best!"

Roma, born in Rome, is the earliest foreign pet to come to "The Peaceable Kingdom," arriving in 1909. From London we welcome Rags and Pekingnese Yente; Medorut from far-away Bucharest, and Bugs, who lived twenty-two years, was born in France.

Foreign influences are evident throughout, and while we don't know all who were born across the sea, we do know that there are strong connections to the homelands. Perhaps a pet's family, continuing a tradition of their own origins, inspired them to engrave many different languages on their pet's monument. It doesn't take long when wandering through "The Peaceable Kingdom" to see this everywhere! Chinese characters, Hieroglyphics, and words like "La Buena," "Siempre," "Jolie," "Toujours," "Amico," "Estaras," "Adorad Compañerito," "Zuckerpuppe" and "Mein." Without question there is a large international community represented at Hartsdale: Chinese, Japanese, Egyptian, Spanish, Germans, Russians and French, just to mention a few.

Quite often we will see religious ceremonies performed by ministers, priests and rabbis. Moreover, there are many monuments and statues honoring Jesus and the saints. There is even a monument engraved with a Cross and a Star of David. An ultimate

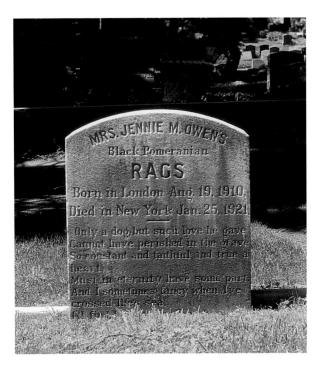

expression of "The Peaceable Kingdom" as a place of ecumenical freedom.

As my wanderings continue, I note other trends and themes from the world at large, engravings that cover everything from space exploration, heavenly bodies, alcoholic beverages and royalty to literary firgues.

Sputnik, for instance, was born in 1957 and named in honor of the historic Russian space flight of that year. Other than man made wonders of the heavens, we meet Luna, Comet, Star, Galaxy, Sunshine and Lily "...who was not the sunshine, was not the sunset, she was the sun."

I wonder why so many pets are named after various liquors. Years ago my dog, Wickets, developed a love for beer, but I suspect that these pets denote more about their owners. In any event, "The Peaceable Kingdom" has a well-stocked liquor cabinet, including Whiskey, Drambuie, Brandy, Champagne, Bourbon, Vodka, Martini and Daiquiri. Even a Pepsi-Cola.

Pets are sometimes named after physical attributes such as courage, power, beauty and strength.

I met one of these majestic dogs and his trainers one day at the cemetery, and I have been touched by something he told me. Speaking of the deep determination of these dogs, he related that when no living people were found for long periods, the dogs would become very depressed. To combat this, several rescuers were purposely buried among the shattered beams and cement so the dogs could find them and experience the joy of saving another life. In truth, I think that all of our pets are heroes and heroines in one way or another, and I pay homage to mine as well as all of the others who share this land.

Every society has its celebrities and "The Peaceable Kingdom" is no exception. Since its beginnings, the cemetery has welcomed famous people who brought their pets here, and many non-celebrities who came with pets who had achieved fame on their own.

Among the famous pets are champions Bambiedoke and Terence of Sunny Slopes who earned titles at the ultimate dog show, the Westminster, held annually in Madison Square Garden in New York City. Bambi, a best of winners appeared in national magazines, and

Terence was so outstanding that he was officially selected as the perfect standard for Saint Bernards.

Champion Brian O'Rourke was known for a devil-may-care attitude, gazing at judges with disdain, raising his leg at the wrong time and going through his "showing" with such a carefree sense of humor that it was reported many a bewildered judge was heard to mutter, "I don't know how to score this dog." However, Briney could not be denied. In addition to a long list of honors, he was the first Kerry blue in the United States and second of his breed to win the Utility Dog championships.

The intoxicating effect of a pet's love has motivated many to name their companion after a favorite cocktail.

Far from the arenas of competion were the pets who became household names as fashion models, stage, screen and television stars. Just to name a few, "The Peaceable Kingdom" is now home to Storm, a handsome German Shepherd who "acted" in such popular TV programs as "Police Story," "Bonanza" and "Ironsides;" Sir, a matinee idol Yorkshire Terrier, who posed for some of the world's most renowned photographers, appeared in top publications including The New York Times Magazine, Vogue and Haper's Bazaar; and super-star Mogan, who "upstaged" such stars as Perry Como, Jackie Gleason and Jerry Lewis. Hailed as an equal to Lassie and Rin Tin Tin, Morgan came home to Hartsdale at the age of seventeen with a ceremony filled with fans and eulogies.

Boots, a sickly puppy about to be given up on, was saved by professional dog trainer Bert Rose. The incredible Boots not only thrived, but went on to become one of Hollywood's most prolific movie stars. During World War II he appeared in USO tours, helped sell millions in war bonds, and was summoned to give command performances for President Franklin D. Roosevelt. Boots' rags-to-riches story could match any of today's "tell-all" biographies. At the height of his career, he earned three thousand dollars a week. He understood hundreds of words and got stage directions correct each time. Boots was incredible and unforgettable and, when he died in the 1950s, obituaries appeared in newspapers throughout the nation. One of these obituaries read in part:

"Boots, veteran film star credited with selling nine million dollars worth of war bonds during the war, will be buried at Hartsdale, N.Y. Canine Cemetery at 11 A.M. tomorrow with a host of Hollywood friends attending. Boots, sixteen, died Friday of a stroke at a Bronx animal hospital. Raised by trainer Bert Rose of Hollywood, the dog appeared in over a dozen pictures and was awarded an Oscar for his performance in Paramount's Emergency Squad."

Celebrities have been coming to Hartsdale for more than eighty years, and while some of their names are not known to later generations, they were as famous in their time as the stars we know today.

In my wanderings, and while doing research, one celebrity stood out in my mind for accomplishments not connected with her legendary career. I speak of internationally famous dancer Irene Castle, who with her husband, Vernon, were the rage of the 20s. Inventors of the popular Castle Walk and Hesitation Waltz, two dance crazes of the time, their every move was news.

Three generations at "The Peaceable Kingdom."

This thought reflects the feelings that many who come to "The Peaceable Kingdom" have for their pets.

Some consider their pets to be <u>loyal</u> friends, while to others they are their <u>best</u> friends and, sadly, to a few they are their <u>only</u> friend.

The sun, the moon and the stars are common astrological themes that pet-owners assimilate to their companions.

In a very unusual way Irene Castle advanced the cause of animals. She was a leading activist in the antivivisection movement and was so appalled that animals suspected of having rabies were destroyed, she made headlines when she volunteered to be bitten by a mad dog, wagering five thousand dollars that she wouldn't contact rabies. She also established the still active "Orphans of the Storm" animal shelter near Chicago. One of her dogs at Hartsdale, Zowie, was depicted in the 1939 Ginger Roger-Fred Astaire movie, "The Story of Irene and Vernon Castle." Irene Castle also buried her pet monkey, Rastas, at "The Peaceable Kingdom." She wrote that Rastas was "the smartest and most lovable monkey that ever lived."

Last, but not least, "The Peaceable Kingdom" has been the chosen place for the pets of many human celebrities. Some are known, others remained anonymous to avoid publicity during their final farewells.

However, while wandering through "The Peaceable Kingdom," I found a virtual "who's who" of well-known men and women. Some may have been forgotten by now; others are still remembered and active. I doubt, for instance, that anyone knows Primrose and West, but they were an acclaimed minstrel team in the 19th century and their pet, Babe, was one of the cemetery's earliest citizens. We know this from the 1902 monument, enhanced with a sculpture of a dog and toy ball.

With too many to mention, here is a partial list of celebrities you will find when you wander through "The Peaceable Kingdom:" from the world of the stage, motion pictures and television: George Raft, Barbara Bennett, Gloria De Haven, Barry Gray, Edwin C. Hill, Evelyn Nesbitt, Dagmar, Florence Reed, Kate Smith, Herb Shriner and television's "Magic Chef" Jack MacPherson,

The tallest monument was erected in 1926 to commemorate Grumpy.

An Ivy League pet?

"Rover's" sister?

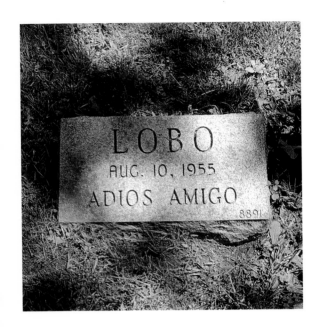

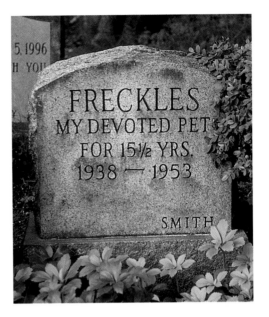

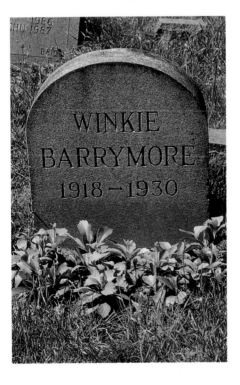

Many celebrities have buried their pets at Hartsdale: Lobo was the pet of McKinley Kantor, author of the Civil War epic, "Andersonville"; singer and early television personality Kate Smith brought Freckles to "The Peaceable Kingdom;" and Jerk and Susie were owned and loved by bandleader/drummer Gene Krupa.

who is buried, along with his wife, with their "beloved pets." Classical musicians Howard Barlow, Frieda Hempel, Fritz Kreisler and Robert Merrill have also buried pets at Hartsdale. From business and finance we have Elizabeth Arden and the infamous millionaire, Heey Green, whose dog is aptly named, Money. We also see the names of sports figures Ralph Kiner and Joe Garagiola, and Pulitzer Prize winner McKinley Kantor, author of *Andersonville*. He also wrote a book titled "Lobo" in honor of his dog who is at Hartsdale. Band leaders Gene Krupa and Xavier Cugat have pets here, as have former New York City Mayor Jimmy Walker and former Vice-President of the United States, James S. Sherman.

This journey through my beloved "Peaceable Kingdom" is nearing its end, but I want to tell you about a wonderful recent addition that has become one of my favorite places to visit.

But, before we go there, I would like to underscore that this new place came about because of a tradition that has guided the cemetery since its beginning: the sensitivity that has made "The Peaceable Kingdom" the foremost resting place for pets in the world. As always, the guardians of the Hartsdale Pet Cemetery have been in the forefront of change since becoming the first place to meet the needs of grief-stricken pet-owners.

Now "The Peaceable Kingdom" has recognized a growing need and as always has filled it. I am speaking of the growing popularity of cremation that many of us are choosing for ourselves as well as our pets. In keeping with this, the Hartsdale Pet Cemetery has created a modern, tasteful way to achieve individual as well as communal pet cremations in a state-of-the-art crematory cradled in a chapel-like building.

Interestingly, dozens of pet owners have chosen cremation through the years so they could be with their pets in "The Peaceable Kingdom."

This leads me back to the place I choose to end my wanderings. It is the cemetery's new Memorial Flower Garden, located near the stately iron gateway to "The Peaceable Kingdom." I consider this magnificent place a "Garden of Eden." As defined by the dictionary, the "Garden of Eden" is a "delightful place; a paradise. A state of innocence of ultimate happiness." Honestly, I couldn't describe this wondrous garden any better.

Edward Way loved his pet so much that he elected to have his cremated remains buried with his beloved Bibi.

Those of us who prefer cremation have a choice of having our pet's ashes lovingly scattered in this lovely place where it can become one with nature.

Even if your pet is not part of the "Garden of Eden," I suggest you pay a visit. For I find this magical place a wonderful spot to sit, relax and reflect. To me this "Garden of Eden" is another reminder of "The Peaceable Kingdom's" very essence: serene, dignified and a symbol of love and care.

Sadly, I have had to make a sad journey to "The Peaceable Kingdom" four times since I wrote my book. Today, my pets live under a magnificent monument, engraved with their family name, ROSYWICK.

As we have seen, there have been many ageless traditions and wonderful new changes at "The Peaceable Kingdom." All of the changes—and those in the planning stages—have enriched the land to new heights. More land has been added; new services, including the dignified crematorium, a nature preserve and the memorial garden and park are offered to all of us. I am confident that "The Peaceable Kingdom" will greet the 21st century with more life than ever before.

There is an old 19th century French saying, which I have always loved, even though I must admit, I never quite understood. It is "Plus ca change, plus c'est la meme chose" – **"The more things change, the more they remain the same."** Now this quotation has been defined for me as I wandered. For while exciting changes are taking place, the basic ideals and exemplary attention to our pets stay the same.

Therefore, it is gratifying to me that I can still repeat the words that ended my book. They mean even more to me now than they did when they first appeared in 1983:

"Today at the cemetery cats, snakes, dogs, hamsters, alligators, chickens, gerbils, rabbits, turtles, pigs, goldfish, mice, pigeons, guinea pigs and the lion 'Goldenfleck', continue to 'live' in a world of love and peace. And with them still, are the trees and flowers, ageless rocks, lush grass, darting insects, and birds and small animals that visit at night .

This is the way it has been, the way it is, the way it will always be.

This is the 'Peaceable Kingdom in Hartsdale.'"

DEDICATED
TO THE MEMORY OF
THE WAR DOG
ERECTED BY PUBLIC CONTRIBUTION
BY DOG LOVERS. TO MAN'S MOST
FAITHFUL FRIEND. FOR THE VALIANT
SERVICES RENDERED IN THE
WORLD WAR
1914 — 1918

A Tribute and Vision
The War Dog Memorial

by Michael G. Lemish
author of *War Dogs–Canines in Combat*

"Dedicated to the memory of the war dog.
Erected by public contribution by dog lovers to man's
faithful friend for the valiant
services rendered in the World War, 1914 - 1918."

At Hartsdale Pet Cemetery, as you ascend the steps leading from North Central Park Avenue up the hillside your eyes are immediately drawn to a granite memorial topped with the bronze image of a shepherd. Although grave markers flank the statue on either side and beyond, the visitor is immediately pulled to this display. As a point of reference in this sprawling cemetery it is simply called the War Dog Memorial.

The likeness of the shepherd, lean and wearing Red Cross markings, can evoke many feelings. What struck me first are the eyes, as the dog seems to gaze beyond you, searching, looking for something or someone – a dog in the midst of his work.

People react to a monument in different ways and to know the background of the War Dog Memorial is to better understand a vision, not of just a war a long time ago but a glimpse into the future.

Dogs have participated in warfare alongside humans since the beginning of recorded history. On a grand time line then, World War I, once known as the "Great War," occurred just a scant moment ago. It took place between 1914 and 1918, involving mostly Europe, eventually the United States, and was the first great conflict of the 20th Century.

A horrific war, it left in its wake over eight million dead, including 100,000 Americans. Canines played an important role, one obscured by the scale of the conflict and, of course, the passage of time. Over 50,000 dogs participated and at least 7,000 were killed. Americans had no canine program, relying instead upon the British and French for military dogs. Red Cross dogs saved thousands of soldiers. Working under the cloak of darkness, they skirted barb wire, deadly mustard and phosgene gas and artillery shelling. They searched in "No Man's Land," ignoring the dead and looking for men still alive. Their heroics on the fields of battle became legendary.

Alexander Pope's painting, which is located at the American Red Cross Museum in Washington D.C., depicts a Red Cross dog returning with a helmet in its mouth. This signifies that the dog has located someone who is wounded. Also note the drifting mustard gas in the background, a nightmarish vision many soldiers faced during World War I.

During the Great War, dogs were also employed as sentries, pulled machine guns and ambulance carts, ran telephone wire, and carried messenger pidgeons. Messenger dogs were also used in large quantities and are indirectly responsible for saving thousands of lives.

Unfortunately, few records were maintained on the accomplishments of these wonderful animals and others disappeared over a period of time. Monuments like the War Dog Memorial help preserve an important part of canine history.

During and immediately after the war, many Americans knew of the amazing success of the war dogs in Europe. The emotional ties binding us to dogs surfaced during this war as Americans learned more about the Red Cross and other military working dogs. This could be seen on the cemetery grounds as Hartsdale grew rapidly during the war years and by 1918 there were over 2,000 graves. An enlightened public, spurred by a group of plot owners, felt a commemoration was necessary for these valiant dogs that served in battle.

The original proposal, a tall obelisk arisen from a broad square base, supported two dogs on the alert. Deemed too radical at the time, a competition was held to choose a final design. Robert Caterson, involved with the building of Grand Central Station and a distant relative of Edward C. Martin, Sr., was chosen to launch the project. Caterson ordered granite from his own quarry in Vermont and created a ten-foot high monument.

The shepherd dog is wearing a Red Cross blanket with a helmet and canteen by his feet. These items are of significant value for the casual on-looker. Red Cross dogs usually carried water or spirits that the wounded could partake of when found. Upon finding a wounded soldier the dog retrieved an item from the person, usually a helmet, and brought this back to his handler. This signified to the handler that someone, alive, had been found. Our shepherd cast in this memorial has done his job, as he looks out to search for someone else in need of help.

So with a culmination of contributions and patriotic spirit, the War Dog Memorial was proudly dedicated in

1923. A simple yet eloquent inscription reads, *"Dedicated to the memory of the war dog. Built by public contributions by dog lovers, to man's most faithful friend, for the valiant services rendered in the world war, 1914–1918."*

It must have been quite an event at the time. Had the onlookers been able to look into the future they may have altered the inscription, casting aside the description of the world war as "the war to end all wars." No one could conceive that twenty-three years later another great conflict would engulf the United States and the world, and that dogs would again enter battle alongside men. So perhaps the Red Cross dog immortalized in bronze is not only casting eyes toward the wounded but what is destined to come.

The Soldier's Friend is a World War I morale boosting poster depicting a Red Cross rescue dog and nurse.

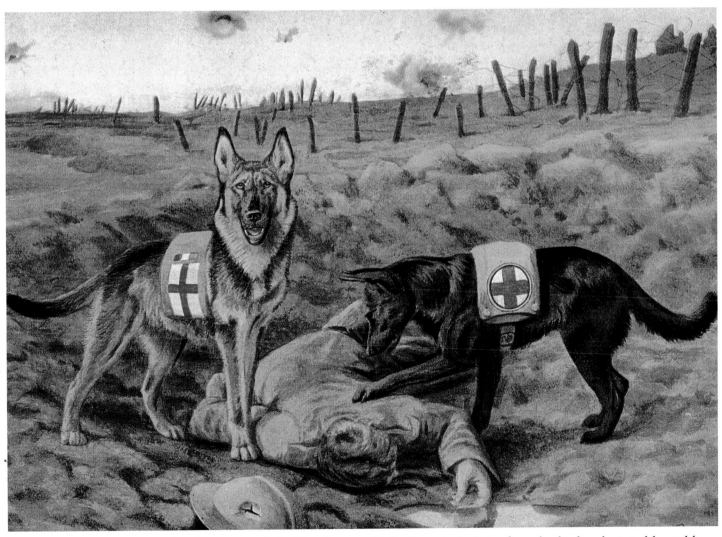

Two Red Cross dogs are shown locating a wounded soldier. Dogs could discriminate the living from the dead and reputedly could distinguish enemy and friendly soldiers.

When the United States entered World War II immediately after the attack on Pearl Harbor, the entire military possessed merely 50 sled dogs. A woman with a vision saw not just an opportunity but a true need to press dogs into service. Alene Erlanger, a dog breeder and fancier, launched a civilian organization called Dogs For Defense and asked Americans to donate their dogs for the war effort.

The need was so great to begin with that thirty-two different breeds were acceptable, although time and experience found several to possess the qualities required by the military. Besides the sled dogs, German Shepherds, Doberman pinchers, and collies proved to be most suited. About 9,000 dogs saw service with the Coast Guard as sentries along the nation's coastlines.

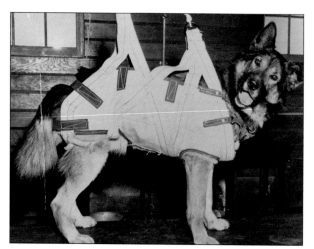

Getting fitted for a parachute harness.

Laying wire during a chemical gas attack.

An American attack took place on November 1, 1943 against the Japanese stronghold on Bouganville in the Solomon Island chain. The assault also included the First Marine War Dog Platoon. Dogs often distinguish themselves during the course of battle and this one was to be no exception.

With tropical downpours and thick vegetation communication by radio was often difficult during the first few days of the campaign. Caesar, a messenger dog, made nine official runs, carrying messages and captured Japanese papers, often through enemy fire.

Like many of the other dogs in the platoon, Caesar also doubled as a sentry at night. On one occasion, while one of his handlers, PFC Rufus Mayo slept, he alerted to an unseen enemy. In the firefight that ensued Caesar caught a sniper's bullet close to the heart. He disappeared but was later found with his second handler, PFC John Kleeman.

Several Marines rigged a stretcher and took turns carrying the wounded dog to the regimental first-aid station. Caesar pulled through with the extra weight of a bullet in his chest and was back on duty three weeks later. Look closely at the photograph and you'll see the bullet wound behind his left shoulder blade.

Other roles developed and dogs learned to become scouts and messengers.

No longer did men face each other from trenches with stagnant front lines, so casualty locators, the Red Cross dogs from World War I, faded from the scene. Unofficially, the military dog program became known as the "K-9 Corps" a term that has remained to this day in the eyes of the public.

Of the 40,000 dogs eventually donated, 12,000 would finally be accepted for military service. Among the more famous was Chips, a shepherd-husky-collie cross who singlehandedly attacked an Italian machine gun post forcing several soldiers to surrender. Chips would soon earn the Purple Heart and Silver Star, human awards that were later revoked. Unlike other countries, the United States has yet to create an award for military working dogs.

At the end of the war, the Army and Marines detrained thousands of dogs, returning them either to their owners, handlers or citizens who had requested a K-9 veteran. It seemed everyone wanted one, and Dogs For Defense received letters requesting war dogs for years, even after all the dogs had been placed.

The experiences of World War II favored the German Shepherd as the most suitable breed for working in a military environment. Just a few years later army scout dog platoons entered into action again during the Korean conflict. One dog named York accompanied men on over 125 different patrols with no casualties. The Army studied the use of scout dogs and found that they averted casualties by at least 65% when leading patrols.

Okinawa – 1945. Members of the 45th Infantry Scout Dog Platoon take a break. During World War II scout dogs were found to be most effective in the Pacific theatre of operations.

1918 – Stubby, the "Hero Dog of WWI" participated in 17 battles and alerted Americans to an impending gas attack.

1952 – York leads 125 patrols against Chinese communists without the single loss of a man during the Korean War.

1966 – Nemo, wounded in the eye, repelled attackers at Tan Son Nhut Air Base, South Vietnam and saved his handler's life.

For a soldier, a dog did not represent a weapon, but a trusted companion with many unique capabilities. Everyone knows that dogs have a powerful sense of smell, termed the olfactory ability, but just how great it is has yet to be determined. Not only can they smell much better than humans, but they can discriminate and associate these odors. Every human gives off their own individual scent, just like a signature.

Acute hearing is another trademark. And although dogs do not see better than humans during the day, they do at night. Being closer to the ground they have an entirely different view than their handlers who stand above them. Powerful jaw muscles, an unabiding loyalty and a deep well of courage, combine to make for a powerful ally. Decades may pass and soldiers may forget many people, but no one ever forgets the dog they went into battle with. With all the technological advances that we have made, it is interesting to note that none of them have completely replaced the unique capabilities that dogs offer us.

After World War II and Korea, the military demobilized much of their working dog program. Ten years later our ardor for warfare would again surface forcing our four-legged companions into battle once more. Vietnam proved that technology could not displace the unique capability of military dogs. More than 3,000 dogs were employed by both the Americans and South Vietnamese. They guarded airbases, led patrols, tracked the enemy and located booby-traps and mines. As a historian and upon review of the facts, I have concluded that dogs helped to avert at least 10,000 casualties during the brutal conflict. Little has been written about the dogs and their handlers who have served in Vietnam. The reason may be that Vietnam drove a wedge between so many Americans. It was definitely a war that asked so much from a few and little from anyone else.

Military working dogs have to be able to tolerate all types of climate. Operations could take place in the cold artic or a Saudi Arabian desert.

Although many breeds were first accepted during World War II, the German Shepherd proved to be the most desirable. Their double-coat can withstand the coldest temperatures and once they loose their inside coat of fine fur, they can adapt to hot tropical climates.

As air sniffing dogs they were most often employed as scouts or sentries. During the Vietnam war, Black Labrador Retrievers served as trackers. In recent years, the Air Force began utilizing the Belgian Malinois for patrols and the detection of explosives and narcotics.

Unlike their civilian counterparts, handlers and military dogs spend just a brief time together – usually months, often just a few weeks. The time line of human and canine intersect for a short-lived moment, yet provide a lifetime of memories.

Rebel was born in 1965 and two years later he was accepted as a scout dog and assigned the number M421. He trained with the 58th Infantry Platoon Scout Dog IPSD at Fort Benning and arrived in South Vietnam in February 1968 while a ground attack took place as part of the Tet offensive. Within six months he was separated from his first handler, PFC Bobby Shaffer, who was wounded in action.

Sgt. Robert Kollar arrived in-country in September 1968 and was assigned to the 58th. "I remember seeing this tan and white animal," Kollar says. "I thought that dog was beautiful, although I never said that to anyone." Sure enough Kollar was assigned Rebel and the two of them became an inseparable team. Nine months later, Kollar was given other duties and moved on. Rebel stayed, a duty given to military dogs as he accepted a new handler. One wonders if dogs ever forget their former masters.

During the war canine cemeteries were constructed throughout South Vietnam. It is here that American dogs that died in the course of their duties were laid to rest by those who worked with them. On September 6, 1969, Rebel died of heat stroke at Camp Evans. Like thousands of other dogs, he lives on within the hearts of his former masters.

We have asked much of dogs since the time the War Dog Memorial was erected. The capabilities of war dogs widened and the tasks given to them appeared endless. Today we also rely on dogs to guide the blind, detect narcotics and explosives, aid police departments and firefighters in arson investigation and lead search and rescue efforts. Too often we just take their work for granted.

For years a man known only as Arthur would visit the War Dog Memorial every Memorial Day. Alone, without bands, twenty-one gun salutes, or applause, he laid a simple wreath at the base. Did this man know something overlooked by everyone else? What compelled him to this act every year? It was in 1974 that a local newspaper reporter caught up with Arthur. As it turned out he was a veteran from the Battle of the Bulge and simply dedicated himself to honor his fallen canine comrades. Obviously a dog, whether in war or peace, had truly touched the soul of this man.

How others came to remember the dogs that have participated in all conflicts would change significantly in later years. Commander Thaddeus Ogden of American Legion Post 8 in New Rochelle, New York, stepped forward. Commander Ogden, with a special resolution in his post's bylaws, ensured that a wreath would be placed at the base of the War Dog Memorial every Memorial Day. Exactly when this took place is not quite known. Since 1992 the Memorial Day ceremony has taken place consistently each year. By no means is the human suffering of these terrible conflicts forgotten, but the past deeds of canine comrades remembered.

In essence the War Dog Memorial has evolved into much more than a commemoration of a war so long ago, a war that has little meaning for anyone today. Our shepherd, cast in bronze, has transcended the pitfall of so many memorials across this great country of ours. Rather than capture just a moment in time, the War Dog Memorial has come to symbolize so much more than a Red Cross dog from a long ago struggle. As a good friend of mine once stated about military dogs, "Here we have a *weapon*, designed by God, to help us save lives." This is truly both the heritage and the future of the war dog.

Hang in there. Marine Corporal Isaiah Martin comforts his dog wounded by a VC sniper, as they await a medevac helicopter in the Que Son Mountains of Vietnam.

Friends to the End
(The history of pet burial)

by Mary Elizabeth Thurston

Not hopeless, round this calm sepulchral spot,
A wreath, presaging life, we twine
If God be love, what sleeps below was not
Without a spark divine.

Epitaph on a Favorite Dog by Sir Francis Hastings Doyle (1810-1888)

The ritualized burial of animals has been practiced in virtually every part of the world at some point in time. In many societies, it was (and still is) a means of honoring animals who endeared themselves to their human families. Such burials stand as enduring expressions of one's emotional affinity with nonhuman beings, and on a more expansive level, one's sense of spiritual kinship with the natural world at large. Funerary rites for animals celebrate the most enduring of human beliefs – that we share the "next life" with other creatures – just as we do this one.

Of all the ancient societies to conduct funerals for animals, Egypt is the best known, thanks to the many elaborately mummified dogs, cats, monkeys and birds that have been recovered by archaeologists in recent times. As early as 1000 B.C., substantial parcels of land along the Nile were set aside expressly for the burial of animals, though it was equally acceptable to inter pets in the tombs of their owners. Wall paintings in these subterranean vaults depict the deceased in scenes from everyday life, and often feature household pets, typically reposed under chairs or dinner tables. Just as spouses and children are labeled by name in many of these portraits, so too are the animals. Names such as Good Herdsman, Reliable, Grabber, Blackie and Useless expressed affection and humor common to many modern dog lovers. Lady, Puss and Sweetie – terms of endearment for favored felines – also have a familiar ring to today's cat enthusiasts.

German funerary procession for a dog, circa 1900.

An ancient Roman grave relief for the female dog, Helena (circa 150-200 A.D.). The "Melitae" (Roman lap dog) sits in a niche under which the inscription reads, "To Helena, foster daughter, imcomparable and praiseworthy soul."

Then as now, wealthy pet-owners spared no expense for their animals' funerals. When a royal guard dog named Abutiu ("With Pointed Ears") died in 2180 B.C., the grieving pharaoh ordered a sarcophagus made for the dog, and that "very much fine cloth, incense and scented oil" be used in the mummification process. It was decreed that Abutiu be interred in his own underground tomb, specially constructed by the royal stone masons, "so that he might become one of the Blessed."

Colorful linen wrappings arranged in ornate herringbone or striped patterns cloaked a dehydrated animal body, which then was finished with a decorative beaded net and gold amulets, or even a finely crafted bronze death mask. Some of these mummies were placed inside cedar or limestone coffins, embellished with hunting scenes and prayers to the gods.

"The limbs of Tamyt, one true of voice before the great god, shall not be weary," reads the sarcophagus inscription for a feline by the same name. The gods, depicted in bas-relief as her pallbearers, suggest that she enjoyed a status equal to humans in mortal life, at least in the eyes of Prince Djehutymose (c.1350 B.C.), her doting owner, who prayed for Tamyt's rebirth as an "imperishable star" in heaven.

Tragically, thousands of Egyptian animal mummies were callously destroyed in the last century by looters seeking gold and precious works of art. British archaeologist E. Naville planned to survey the cat cemetery at Tell Basta (in the southeastern Delta) around 1880, but found it had been pillaged. He sadly noted in his diary that nothing remained but "scattered heaps of white bones." About this time, too, tons of animal mummies were exported to England to be pulverized and sold as garden fertilizer – according to merchant ledgers, one such shipment weighed in excess of nineteen tons and contained 180,000 animals! Fortunately, a small sampling of these mummies were collected by British Museum curators, and today, nondestructive forensic examinations with state-of-the-art diagnostic technologies such as endoscopy and CAT scans hold the promise of a deeper understanding of the ancient human-animal relationship.

A young Greek hunter with his dog was painted on a vase dating from around 460 B.C.

An endearing collared terracotta dog from Mesopotamia, made around 1900 B.C.

Egyptian bronze statuette of a puppy, wearing a gold collar. Eighteenth Dynasty, circa. 1350 B.C.

Frederick the Great (1712-1786) was devoted to his thirteen Italian Greyhounds. His death bed request was to be buried in a crypt (in the gazebo) situated to overlook the little graves of his dogs (foreground). Instead, he was entombed next to his father in Potsdam's Garrison Church. Over the next two centuries, he was exhumed and relocated three times. Finally, in 1991, the royal remains were returned to the palace called Sanssouci ("No Tears"), and in accordance with the king's last wish, laid to rest with the dogs he loved so dearly in life. The tiny skeleton of a dog, probably the last one he owned, was discovered inside the garden crypt when it was opened.

Egypt was contemporary with a number of other pet-keeping societies, of course, notably the seafaring Greeks and Romans, who also honored animals in death, particularly those who distinguished themselves in the service of their masters. Lithe hunting dogs frequently touched the hearts of their sporting owners, as evidenced by one ancient Mediterranean tombstone, which reads:

Thou passest on the path, if happily thou dost mark this monument, Laugh not, I pray thee, Though it is a dog's grave, tears fell for me, and the dust was heaped above me by a master's hand, who likewise engraved these words upon my tomb.

Perhaps the most famous classical dog lover was Alexander the Great (336 B.C.-323B.C.), who owned a large Mastiff-like hound named Peritas. Upon her death, the conqueror led a formal funeral procession to the grave, erected a large stone monument on the site and ordered nearby residents to celebrate her memory in annual festivities. A city by the same name still exists in this location.

Canine devotion and courage sometimes touched the hearts of an entire populace, as in the case of fifty dogs who patrolled the perimeter of Corinth, which one night was the object of a surprise attack. While the soldiers slept, the dogs alone defended the citadel, fighting valiantly until all were killed save one. The citizens erected a marble tribute to the forty-nine dogs who died protecting their town, and Sorter, the lone survivor, was given a pension for life and an engraved silver collar that read, "Sorter, savior of Corinth, placed under the protection of his friends."

Some Victorian pet owners opted to have their beloved animals taxidermied rather than struggle with the difficulty of finding a suitable burial site. These dogs, cats, parrots and monkeys often sat in the parlor or on the fireplace mantle, next to portraits of other deceased members of the family.

After centuries of affiliation with the pagan gods of Egypt, Rome and Greece, many animals were subject to persecution in the new Christian era, starting around 700 A.D. Medieval dogs and cats often were accused of being the consorts of witches, or even worse, were Satan incarnate. There was little tolerance for people who cuddled or talked to animals, and even less for the notion of burying pets with the same pomp and ceremony accorded humans. Still, there were a courageous few who argued that animals were entitled to posthumous honors. As one French cleric arranged a formal Christian funeral for his little dog, news of the plan leaked to his supervising bishop, who demanded that he appear before a tribunal to answer charges of heresy. Amazingly, the priest pleaded his innocence and not only succeeded in getting all charges dropped, but humiliated his accuser as well. "You will understand, my Lord, that I was able to put this dog, who was worth much more than a good number of Christians, in a discreet position," he said to the council. "The dog gave me many instances of wisdom in life, and above all in its death! It even wished to leave me its will, at the head of which is the name of the bishop of this diocese, to whom it bequeaths 150 crowns, which I have here for you now."

Animals belonging to wealthy, influential landowners were usually exempt from such religious persecution. Successive generations of noble pets were lovingly interred in the gardens of many country estates, a tradition that continues in modern times. "His attachment was without selfishness, his playfulness without malice, his fidelity without deceit," reads the epitaph of

This cemetery for mascots and officer's dogs at Edinburgh Castle (Scotland) has been in use since Queen Victoria's reign.

London's Hyde Park Dog's Cemetry, as it appeared at the turn of the century.

Dash the spaniel, the first and perhaps best-loved dog of Princess Victoria, who as Queen (1837-1901) campaigned aggressively for the establishment of a new humane ethic in English society. Over the course of her long life, the vast grounds surrounding Windsor Castle became the final resting place for several beloved horses, one tiny finch, and many dogs, their likenesses immortalized in life-size bronze statues marking the graves.

In the latter half of the nineteenth century, as technological innovation and social reforms revolutionized the standard of living for the working class, companion animals became mainstream fixtures of modern urban life. Many people felt disoriented or left behind by this rapidly changing world, so they turned to their dogs and cats for emotional support. For the single or elderly in particular, animals were the only family, the only "people" they could depend on to love them regardless of their standing (or lack or it) in the community. "Is not the dog an animal that we can exalt without any reservation?" pondered French essayist George Harmois in 1890, echoing the sentiments of the growing ranks of animal lovers in Europe and America. "Is he not worth as much as many men, and more than some others?"

This Hyde Park headstone attests to the bittersweet devotion of a dog.

andless pet-owners living in densely populated cities were confronted with two nightmarish options when an animal died: throwing it out with the trash or placing the body in a weighted sack and flinging it into a nearby river (in 1899 alone, three thousand such pets were pulled from the Seine by Paris sanitation crews). Complaining of the lack of dignified options for saying farewell to an animal, dog enthusiast Charles Burkett pointed out in 1907 that ancient societies honored deceased animals, "while our *advanced* civilization, that knows so much better, casts them into the manure pit." Untold numbers rejected both options, choosing instead to risk arrest by sneaking into municipal parks after dark to inter their dogs and cats — in a sense, public tracts of land such as New York City's Central Park may constitute some of the world's largest (albeit unsanctioned) pet cemeteries.

Entrance to the "Cemetery of Dogs" at Asnières-sur Seine, near Paris.

At Asnières, some pet owners return each season to plant flowers on the graves of their dogs and cats.

Barry the St. Bernard (1804-1816) saved the lives of 40 people lost in the Swiss alps; the 41st person mistook him for a wolf and killed him. This monument was erected at Asnières around 1900.

"In memory of Fred," reads the back of this German photo (circa 1905), apparently referring to the dog in the painting on the wall. To mark the death of a pet, some people had their photos taken at the animal's gravesite, or in this instance, with a portrait made in life. The unnamed woman appears to be wearing the dog's hat.

A few went so far as to sneak into human cemeteries to bury pets in plots reserved for themselves. One such clandestine funeral took place in 1898 in Columbus, Ohio for a dog named Diana, who was laid out in a little white coffin decorated with silver trimmings. "We took carriages at night [to the cemetery], and at the grave recounted the fidelity and true nobility of our canine friend," recalled Mrs. A.J. Chevalier, Diana's owner, who orchestrated the illegal interment with the help of discreet friends.

Little wonder then that the establishment of the first public pet cemeteries on the advent of the twentieth century was welcome news to thousands of animal lovers. Crushed under the wheels of a carriage barreling down busy Bayswater Road, the accidental death in 1888 of Prince, a Dachshund belonging to the Duke of Cambridge, inadvertently led to the creation of a small but extremely popular pet cemetery in the heart of London. Stories of the dog's demise touched the public, and soon other pet-owners were petitioning for permission to bury their dogs in the little fenced garden adjoining the groundskeeper's cottage. Within twelve years it contained more than three hundred graves and had to be closed to further burials.

Other pioneering pet cemeteries sprang up in the last decade of the nineteenth century, some of which offer burial services to this day. Founded in 1899 by feminist Marguerite Durand, the dog cemetery at Asnières lies on a forested river islet near Paris that was already a playground of the middle and professional working class, thereby smoothing its conversion into a charming garden-style resting place for animals. And, of course, there is the Hartsdale Canine Cemetery, the oldest and largest of its kind in America. With its beautifully manicured grounds and creatively crafted grave markers, Hartsdale is among the crown jewels of historic pet cemeteries.

Last rites for Victorian pets could be as formal as any concocted for humans. Supported by sympathetic friends dressed head-to-toe in black, pet owners conducted their own gravesite services, reading Bible excerpts or eulogizing the lives of their dogs. "Zip lay in state in his velvet robe inside a polished walnut coffin, surrounded by a guard of two fox terriers and one bull dog," wrote a

Philadelphia newspaper reporter, who witnessed the funeral of this performing dog in 1898. The salon was filled with flowers, courtesy of Zip's many friends and fans, and after two days of viewing, the dog was interred next to his father, also a canine thespian.

Around the same time, a funeral was conducted at Hartsdale for Major, a highly-trained spaniel said to "sing in three languages," according to his owner. After a period of lying in state wearing a solid gold collar, Major's satin-lined casket, complete with a crystal window in the lid, was draped in flowers and escorted to the cemetery. As a small crowd of friends sang a doxology, he was lowered into the grave.

Some deceased pets were photographed on lace-covered pillows, posed as though they were in blissful slumber (it was customary to photograph deceased children in the same manner), and many owners kept locks of their animal's hair in gold lockets or specially designed rings. One English woman who interred her Pomeranian in a double-locked casket in Hyde Park retained and wore the keys on a chain for the duration of her own life.

Marble dog houses and sculptures of dogs marked the graves of many Victorian pets, as did stone or mortar renderings of more typical romantic images, such as doves, lambs, angels

In 1835, Countess the Bloodhound slipped on her master's second-story balcony, and fell to her death. She was transported to English animal portraitist Edwin Landseer the next morning. Cradling the body in his arms, Landseer told her grieving master to "go away until Thursday." Three days later, the artist persented a finished four-foot canvas to the dog's owner, depicting Countess in peaceful repose. The <u>Sleeping Bloodhound</u>, as this painting came to be known, was reproduced as a steel engraving and sold to the masses. It was one of the most popular dog renderings of the Victorian era.

Memorial plaque to Ringwood the Otterhound, dating from the Eighteenth century at Rousham Manor near Oxford, England.

In front of this Stream lies the Remains of
RINGWOOD
an Otter-Hound of extraordinary Sagacity

Tyrant of the Cherwell's Flood
Come not near this farred Cleam,
Nor with thy unfulting Breed
Dare pollute my RINGWOOD'S Tomb.

What tho Death has laid him low,
Long the terror of thy Race
Couples taught by him to Know,
Taught to force thy lurking Place.

Hark how STUBBORN's airy Tongue
Warns the time to point the Spear
RUFFON loud thy Knoll had rung,
RULER echoes Death is near.

All the Skies in Cosort rend,
BUTLER ohears with highest glee
Still thy Master and thy friend
RINGWOOD ever think of thee.

Molesworth Pet Cemetery as it appears today – in ruins.

and miniature weeping willows. Other people opted for simple headstones inscribed with the animal's name and a short epitaph, conveying emotions shared by grieving pet owners today. Bible verses, excerpts from Shakespearean plays, poetry by Lord Byron or a simple statement of the owner's own creation were popular. "Not one of them is forgotten before God," many stones in Hyde Park solemnly declare. "Drowned in Old Windsor Loch," "poisoned," "run over" and "pined for his mistress" were heart-wrenching commentaries on tragic ends. Many inscriptions are timeless commentaries on the constancy of animals as compared with people, such as the one found on an elaborate pedestal erected over the grave of a French dog around 1890, which reads, "to the memory of my dear Emma — faithful and sole companion of my otherwise rootless and desolate life."

An untold number of pet memorials, some of which date back 200 years or more, still survive on private estates scattered through Europe, but many Victorian animal cemeteries have been destroyed in recent years. As ancestral estates have been liquidated or subdivided for modern development, headstones are uprooted and smashed, or in one instance, relegated to a small island of grass in the middle of a busy English motorway.

Such a tragic fate has befallen the once-posh Molesworth cemetery in Huntingdonshire, England, which at the turn of the century was one of the most ornately decorated animal cemeteries in world, but today stands on the brink of total destruction. The Italian marble columns, arches, sculptures and miniature mausoleums with stained glass windows that once graced this final resting place for Victorian pets have been defaced, demolished or stolen. What grave markers remain can be found at the edge of an open field, many of them face down and half-buried among the overgrown bushes.

With interest growing among scholars and history buffs in the preservation of historic human cemeteries, we can only hope that the notion of protecting pet graveyards will become popular as well — before it is too late.

On the threshold of the twenty-first century, the number of people who regard animals as members of their families continues to grow, as evidenced by the fact that there are now more than five hundred pet cemeteries in the United States alone. The traditional wooden casket and simple stone marker is still popular, although one Utah-based company now offers "Egyptian-style" mummification for both animals and people. After months of immersion in a bath of preservative chemicals, pets are wrapped in fabric strips, arranged in a natural posture, coated in polyethylene resin, and then encased in a life-like sarcophagus, finished in gold leaf, effectively transforming the bodies into sculptures, suitable for home display.

That so many people choose to commemorate the lives of their pets is good news, for it signals a renewed sense of kinship with the natural world, largely inspired by the companion animals who aid and comfort us within the increasingly impersonal confines of our modern society.

"Who can say that this does not betoken the growth and spread of the humanitarian spirit, [especially] in times that try men's souls," remarked a spokesperson for the Massachusetts SPCA in 1900, upon noting the public's growing interest in funerals for pets. Indeed, that so many people choose to honor the lives of their animals in places like Hartsdale points to a revolution taking place in our concept of ourselves — that we are part of the larger world of animals, not above or separate from it — one pet and person at a time.

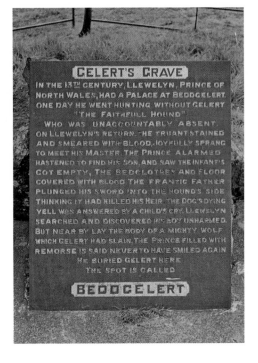

GELERT'S GRAVE
In the 13th century, Llewelyn, Prince of
North Wales, had a Palace at Beddgelert.
One day he went hunting without Gelert
"The Faith Hound"
who was unaccountably absent.
On Llewelyn's return, the truant stained
and smeared with blood, joyfully sprang
to meet his Master. The Prince alarmed
hastened to find his son, and saw the infant's
cot empty, the bedclothes and floor
covered with blood. The frantic father
plunged his sword into the hound's side
thinking it had killed his heir. The dog's dying
yell was answered by a child's cry. Llewelyn
searched and discovered his boy unharmed.
But nearby lay the body of a mighty wolf
which Gelert had slain. The Prince filled with
remorse is said never to have smiled again.
He buried Gelert here.
The spot is called
BEDDGELERT

Epilogue

William Gladstone, Prime Minister of England under Queen Victoria once said, "Show me the manner in which a nation cares for its dead and I will measure with mathematical exactness the tender sympathies of its people, their respect for the law and their loyalty to high ideals." The manner in which we pay our last respects for those we love, whether they are human or animal reflects our sense of the meaning of life, not death. It is a symbol of our most basic instincts. That is why we find ceremonial pet burials five thousand years ago and that is why they will continue as long as there are animal companions and people who love them.

A single compassionate act by a thoughtful veterinarian over one hundred years ago has served as the cornerstone for the first pet cemetery in the United States. The Hartsdale Canine Cemetery is not simply a plot of land set apart for the burial of pet animals. It is a place of such beauty that it has become a perpetual memorial not only for those interred within its boundaries but also to animals throughout the world. It is not a gloomy area that speaks of death, but a place that vibrates with life – of growing things which pass through the cycles of the seasons, bursting forth in the spring of each year into new youth and new vitality.

Anyone who has ever had a pet to love and care for understands how sad it is to say good-bye

Bios

Mary Elizabeth Thurston has devoted her life to campaigning for the compassionate treatment of all creatures. A specialist in the history of human-companion animal relationships, Thurston has curated several traveling exhibits tracing society's growing affinity for pets. She also is a founding member of Animal Trustees of Austin, a Texas-based charity that rescues dogs and cats from "death row" at area pounds. Her writing about her pets have appeared in dozens of magazines, from Good Housekeeping and Dog World, to the Journal of the International Society of Companion Animal Studies. Her book, *The Lost History of the Canine Race*, examines the shared heritage of people and dogs from the Ice Age to the Computer Age. Thurston lives in Austin with her beloved canine, Petey.

Michael Lemish is the official historian for the Vietnam Dog Handler Association and is the author of *War Dogs: Canines in Combat* (Brassey's). He writes for numerous popular, association and trade magazines, including "The American Legion Magazine" and "Boys Life." A member of the National Association for Search and Rescue, Lemish is involved in search-and-rescue activities. He lives in Westborough, Massachusetts, with his wife, son and their golden retriever, "Yeager."

Malcolm D. Kriger, author of "The Peaceable Kingdom in Hartsdale", has had a close personal association with the cemetery since bringing his first dog, Wickets, here in 1969. He decided at that time he wanted to know more about his dog's final resting place, and in the following years he did extensive research and writing for "The Peaceable Kingdom in Hartsdale". Mr. Kriger chose to take full responsibility for publishing the book so it would be exactly as he envisioned it.

Today, his six Cairn Terriers — Wickets, Wick, Min, Rosy, Rocky and Clyde — rest at Hartsdale at the Rosywick monument. He continues to reside and write in New York City where he lives with his Cairn Terrier, Roxy.

Picture Credits